To J.....
From M.a.....
23. 5. 5.....
with all my
love x

'TO A VERY SPECIAL'® AND 'TO-GIVE-AND-TO-KEEP'® ARE
REGISTERED TRADE MARKS OF EXLEY PUBLICATIONS LTD AND
EXLEY GIFTBOOKS.

Other mini books in the series:

To a very Special Dad	To a very Special Sister
To a very Special Daughter	To a very Special Son
To a very Special Friend	To my very Special Wife
To a very Special Granddaughter	Happy Anniversary
To a very Special Grandmother	Welcome to the New Baby
To a very Special Grandpa	Wishing you Happiness
To my very Special Love	Merry Christmas
To my very Special Mother	To a very Special Grandson
To a very Special Teacher	To a Special Couple on your Wedding Day

Published simultaneously in 1992 by Exley Publications Ltd, in Great Britain, and
Exley Giftbooks in the USA.

Illustrations copyright © Helen Exley 1992   Selection copyright © Helen Exley 1992
The moral right of the author has been asserted.

30 29 28 27 26 25 24 23 22 21 20 19 18 17

ISBN 1-85015-264-0 (Laminate edition)
     1-86187-043-4 (Personalised suedel edition)
     1-86187-058-2 (Suedel edition)

A copy of the CIP data is available from the British Library on request.
All rights reserved. No part of this publication may be reproduced or transmitted
in any form or by any means, electronic or mechanical, including photocopy,
recording or any information storage and retrieval system without permission in
writing from the Publisher.

Illustrations by Juliette Clarke
Edited by Helen Exley.

Typesetting by Delta, Watford
Printed in Hungary.

For Richard, with all my love.

Exley Publications Ltd, 16 Chalk Hill, Watford, Herts WD1 4BN, United Kingdom
Exley Publications LLC, 232 Madison Avenue, Suite 1206, NY 10016, USA.

Acknowledgements: The publishers gratefully acknowledge permission to reprint
copyright material. They would be pleased to hear from any copyright holders not
here acknowledged. W.H. Auden, extract from "As I Walked Out One Evening",
from Collected Poems, © 1940 and renewed 1968 by W.H. Auden. Reprinted with
permission of Faber and Faber Ltd & Random House Inc; Oscar Hammerstein II,
extract from "Can't Help Lovin' Dat Man" © reproduced by kind permission of
Polygram Music Publishing Ltd, 347-353 Chiswick High Road, London W4 4HS;
Adrian Henri, extract from "Without You" from Collected Poems, published by
Allison and Busby, 1986 copyright © Adrian Henri, reprinted by permission of
Rogers, Coleridge & White Ltd; James Joyce, extract from Ulysses, published by
The Bodley Head, copyright © 1934 and renewed 1962 by Lucia & George Joyce.
Reprinted by permission of Random House, Inc.

To my very special
HUSBAND

A HELEN EXLEY GIFTBOOK
Illustrations by Juliette Clarke

Keep this little book somewhere
ordinary, where your eyes may fall on it
a dozen times a day. So that, wherever
I am, you will be reminded of me -
and of how much I love you.

. . .

EXLEY
NEW YORK • WATFORD, UK

WHAT IS A HUSBAND?

He is the one the flowers are always from.

TRISHA GOODWIN

. . .

He is the one that makes you feel like having

children - his children.

DIANE YOUNG

. . .

A husband is a man who when someone tells him

he is hen-pecked, answers, yes, but I am pecked

by a good hen.

GILL KARLSEN

. . .

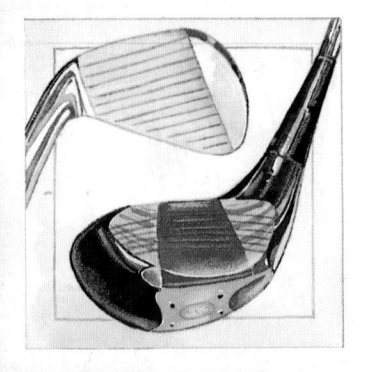

A husband is an expert
at drying in between
tiny toes and fingers.

LYNN CUNNINGHAM

. . .

A husband is the only person whose socks you'd wash without a shudder.

LINDA CORNISH

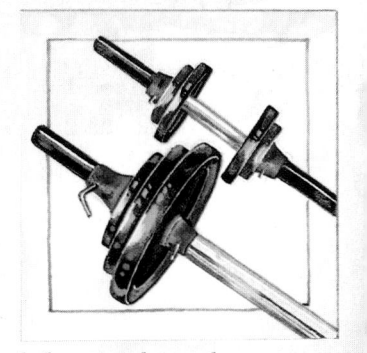

. . .

He is a man who stands by you through all the troubles you wouldn't have had if you had stayed single!

L.M. SMITH

. . .

A husband says "I love you" when you're wearing a face-pack; and remembers your punch-lines for you in public.

JILL WOODS

. . .

He's the guy who makes me say to God every day, "Thanks for this guy, God."

VERONICA CASSIDY

. . .

I CAN'T HELP IT

When I pick the ricefield weeds

With the man I love,

The little weeds behind us

Are still there.

JAPANESE FOLK SONG

. . .

He lights my world with love and laughter. He

gives to all my days the warm promise of Spring,

and because of him I am ever young. So,

Darling, for yesterday, today, and all my tomorrows,

my love and my thanks.

CATHERINE JENKINSON

. . .

...For when I glance at you even an instant, I can no longer utter a word: my tongue thickens to a lump, and beneath my skin breaks out a subtle fire: my eyes are blind, my ears filled with humming, and sweat streams down my body, I am seized by a sudden shuddering; I turn greener than grass, and in a moment more, I feel I shall die.

SAPPHO (c. 612-580 B.C.)

. . .

A husband is the best friend you will ever have in your life. He will share your thoughts, your moods, your laughter and your tears. He is someone to live up to and to follow to the ends of the earth. And if that sounds too sentimental, I can't help it, because that's the way I feel about my husband.

SUSAN HOLMES

. . .

CRAZY WITH LOVE

I know every bump, every bulge, every wrinkle.
Every sag, every bag, every scar, every flaw,
every whisker.
I know that you fleck the bathroom tiles with
shaving foam, that you flood the floor with
bath water, that you never take your plate out
to the sink, that your strew your clothes, that
you forget to change your socks, that you tell
me the endings of detective novels, that you
track mud through the house, that you never
remember to pay the paper bill.
I know your eccentricities, your prejudices,
your moods. And somehow, for some reason I
can never fully understand, I am crazy with
love for you.

CHARLOTTE GRAY, b.1937

. . .

...Fish got to swim and birds got to fly,

I got to love one man till I die,

Can't help lovin' dat man of mine.

Tell me he's lazy, tell me he's slow,

Tell me I'm crazy, maybe I know.

Can't help lovin' dat man of mine!

...When he goes away,

Dat's a rainy day,

An' when he come back dat day is fine,

The sun will shine.

He can come home as late as can be,

Home without him ain't no home to me,

Can't help lovin' dat man of mine!

OSCAR HAMMERSTEIN 2nd
from *"Can't Help Lovin' Dat Man"*

. . .

<u>LOVERS – ALWAYS</u>

A real marriage bears no resemblance to these
marriages of interest or ambition. It is two lovers
who live together. A priest may well say certain
words, a notary may well sign certain papers -
I regard these preparations in the same way
that a lover regards the rope ladder that he ties
to his mistress's window.

LADY MARY WORTLEY MONTAGU (1689-1762)

...and then I asked him with my eyes and then he

asked me would I yes...and first I put my arms

around him yes

and drew him down to me to ask again yes

so he could feel my breasts all perfume yes

and his heart was going like mad

and yes I said yes I will Yes.

JAMES JOYCE (1882-1941)
from *"Ulysses"*

. . .

At Kataushika the river water

Runs gently, and the plum blossom

Bursts out laughing.

The nightingale cannot withstand so many joys

And sings, and we are reconciled.

Our warm bodies touch,

Cane branch and pine branch,

Our boat floats in toward the bank.

from *"Song of the Geishas"*

. . .

When you are away
too long I put on
your ancient
gardening jacket
and sit wrapped
round in you.

PAM BROWN, b.1928

. . .

WITHOUT YOU

In the arithmetic of love, one plus one equals
everything, and two minus one equals nothing.

MIGNON McLAUGHLIN

. . .

One of the oldest human needs is having someone
to wonder where you are when you don't come
home at night.

MARGARET MEAD (1901-1978)

. . .

Without you every morning would be like

going back to work after a holiday,...

Without you every musician in the world

would forget how to play the blues,

Without you Public Houses would be

public again,...

Without you all streets would be one-way

the other way,...

Without you there'd be no one not to kiss

goodnight when we quarrel,...

ADRIAN HENRI
from *"Without You"*

. . .

I spread out the days before me - the days we have

spent together - some bright as frosty stars, some

glowing with an opalescent magic, some cool as

water-tumbled pebbles, some flashing with fire.

What would they have been without you?

Dates crossed off on a calendar.

MARION C. GARRETTY, b.1917

. . .

I'D DO ANYTHING

Gladly I'll live in a poor mountain hut,

Spin, sew, and till the soil in any weather,

And wash in the cold mountain stream, if but

We dwell together.

JAPANESE LYRIC

. . .

Lady Bird would crawl down Pennsylvania Avenue

on cracked glass for Lyndon Johnson.

JACQUELINE KENNEDY ONASSIS, b.1929
from *"The Tragedy of Lyndon Johnson"*

. . .

It was during the period of martial law. The middle of June of last year. She was seeing me for the first time since our arrest, after six weeks of suffering spent in solitude in her cell, brooding over reports that announced my death. They called her in to soften me up.

"Talk to him," the division chief said to her on confronting her with me. "Urge him to be reasonable. If he won't think of himself, he might at least think of you. You still have an hour to think it over. If he is still obdurate after that, you will be shot tonight. Both of you."

She caressed me with her glance and answered simply: "Officer, that's no threat for me, that's my last wish: If you are going to kill him, Kill me too."

JULIUS FUCIK (1903-1943)
from notes made during his imprisonment by the Gestapo

. . .

BOUND TO EACH OTHER

Campaigners against [marriage], from Shelley and the Mills on, have been remarkably crass in posing the simple dilemma, "either you want to stay together or you don't - if you do, you need not promise, if you don't, you ought to part." This ignores the chances of inner conflict, and the deep human need for a continuous central life that lasts through genuine, but passing, changes of mood. The need to be able to rely on other people is not some sort of shameful weakness; it is an aspect of the need to be true to oneself.

MARY MIDGLEY
from *"Beast and Man"*

. . .

Why do people stay together? Putting aside "for the sake of the children", and "the habit of years" and "economic reasons" as lawyers' nonsense - it's not much more...it's because they can't; they are bound. And nobody on earth knows what are those bonds that bind them except those two.

KATHERINE MANSFIELD (1888-1923)

. . .

Perhaps recognition comes after an affair, following disgrace in business, or simple low-level crime; maybe one partner cannot cope; sometimes it might be illness and attendant ill-humour... all these can be accommodated.... The cynic might say that partners "accommodate" each other because they are afraid of isolation. I prefer to imagine that the "injured" partner sees weakness and need in the other's face - then peers in the mirror to see the same, turning back to forgive.

BEL MOONEY
from *"From This Day Forward"*

. . .

TO MY DEAR AND LOVING HUSBAND

If ever two were one, then surely we.

If ever man were lov'd by wife, then thee.

If ever wife was happy in man,

Compare with me, ye women, if you can.

I prize thy love more than whole mines of gold,

Or all the riches that the East doth hold.

My love is such that rivers cannot quench,

Nor ought but love from thee give recompence.

Thy love is such I can no way repay;

The heavens reward thee manifold I pray.

Then while we live, in love let's so persevere,

That when we live no more, we may live ever.

ANNE BRADSTREET (c.1612-1672)

. . .

You are the memory of a dappled pool in the
Drakensburg mountains
You are the strong arms that protect me
through the night.
You are the roses that grow tall and free
in my garden.
You are the man who gave me my two
beautiful sons.
You are the seven-year-old who asks me if I can give
him endless affection.
You are the shoulder pains that need my soothing
hands and voice.
You are the sound of Vivaldi singing through the
years that are my life.
You are the colleague whose advice I always respect.
You.
No wonder I love you.

HELEN THOMSON, b.1943

. . .

MARRIED LOVE

When two people are at one in their inmost hearts,

They shatter even the strength of iron or of bronze.

And when two people understand each other in

their inmost hearts,

Their words are sweet and strong, like the fragrance

of orchids.

I-CHING

. . .

Familiar acts are beautiful through love.

PERCY BYSSHE SHELLEY (1792-1817)
from *"Prometheus Unbound"*

. . .

Love doesn't just sit there, like a stone, it

has to be made, like bread; remade all

the time, made new.

URSULA K. LE GUIN

. . .

A happy marriage is the best thing life has to offer. It

is built up brick by brick over the years and

cemented as much by the moments of tenderness as

by those of irritation.

JILLY COOPER

. . .

A successful marriage is not a gift;

it is an achievement.

ANN LANDERS, b.1918

. . .

WE TWO

You and I

Have so much love,

That it burns like a fire,

In which we bake a lump of clay

Molded into a figure of you

And a figure of me.

Then we take both of them,

And break them into pieces,

And mix the pieces with water,

And mold again a figure of you,

And a figure of me.

I am in your clay.

You are in my clay.

In life we share a single quilt.

In death we will share one coffin.

KUAN TAO-SHENG (13th century A.D.)

. . .

In the end they knew each other so well that by the time they had been married for thirty years they were like a single divided being, and they felt uncomfortable at the frequency with which they guessed each other's thoughts without intending to, or the ridiculous accident of one of them anticipating in public what the other was going to say. Together they had overcome the daily incomprehension, the instantaneous hatred, the reciprocal nastiness and fabulous flashes of glory in the conjugal conspiracy. It was the time when they loved each other best, without hurry or excess, when both were most conscious of and grateful for their incredible victories over adversity. Life would still present them with other mortal trials, of course, but that no longer mattered: they were on the shore.

GABRIEL GARCIA MARQUEZ
from *"Love in the Time of Cholera"*

. . .

FOR LIFE

Even after fifteen years it's like eating soup with a fork, I just can't get enough of him.

JOANNE JONES

. . .

To be allowed to grow old together, to continue to need and to feed one another, "and the years forgot", must be every couple's hope.

HELGE RUBINSTEIN

. . .

Marriage was only the beginning. The lines of our loving weave an ever more closely patterned fabric – a tapestry of a shared life.

PAM BROWN

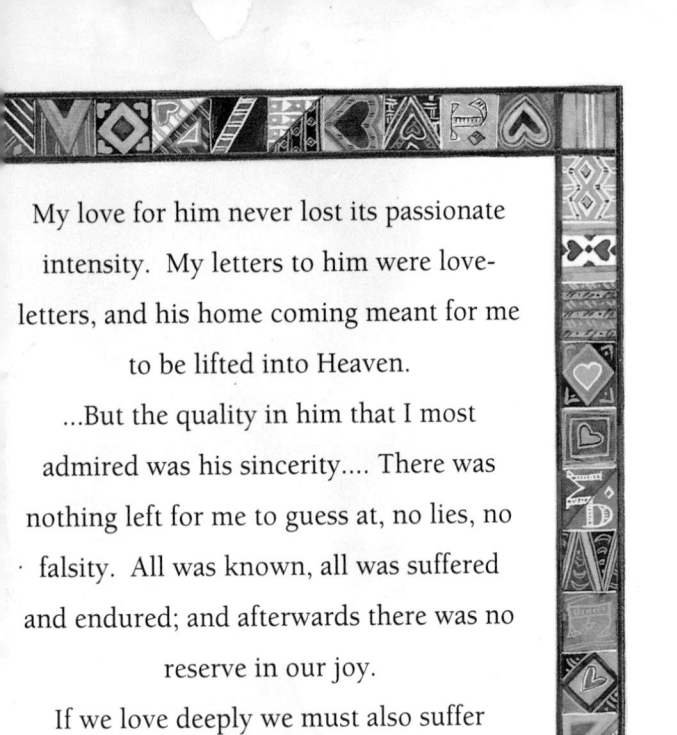

My love for him never lost its passionate intensity. My letters to him were love-letters, and his home coming meant for me to be lifted into Heaven.

...But the quality in him that I most admired was his sincerity.... There was nothing left for me to guess at, no lies, no falsity. All was known, all was suffered and endured; and afterwards there was no reserve in our joy.

If we love deeply we must also suffer deeply; for the price for the capacity for ecstatic joy is anguish. And so it was with us to the end.

HELEN THOMAS

MY EVERYTHING

My husband is humble and when he says,
"Why do you love me? I am so ordinary", it
hurts because I can never find the words to tell
him he is my whole world.

V.M. HALES

. . .

Your presence pervades the house. Even when you
are away I find myself listening for you. I open every
door, half expecting to find you there – turn to
speak and feel my heart die a little in the silence.
You are in my mind and in my heart. You are in the
very air I breathe. You are part of me. Forever.

ROSANNE AMBROSE-BROWN, b.1943

. . .

I love thee with the breath, smiles, tears,

of all my life!

ELIZABETH BARRETT BROWNING (1806-1861)

. . .

I'll love you dear, I'll love you

Till China and Africa meet,

And the salmon sing in the street.

I'll love you till the ocean

Is folded and hung up to dry

And the seven stars go squawking

Like geese about the sky.

W.H. AUDEN (1907-1973)
from *"As I walked out one evening"*

. . .